AF575846

AUSTRALIA

Tracy Vonder Brink

TABLE OF CONTENTS

A Crabtree Seedlings Book

Crabtree Publishing
crabtreebooks.com

School-to-Home Support for Caregivers and Teachers

This book helps children grow by letting them practice reading. Here are a few guiding questions to help the reader with building his or her comprehension skills. Possible answers appear here in red.

Before Reading:

- What do I think this book is about?
  - *I think this book is about Australia.*
  - *I think this book is about the people of Australia.*

- What do I want to learn about this topic?
  - *I want to learn more about the animals that live in Australia.*
  - *I want to learn about the weather in Australia.*

During Reading:

- I wonder why...
  - *I wonder how big the Great Barrier Reef is.*
  - *I wonder why the largest land area in Australia is called the Outback.*

- What have I learned so far?
  - *I have learned that Australia has many beautiful beaches.*
  - *I have learned that Sydney is the biggest city in Australia.*

After Reading:

- What details did I learn about this topic?
  - *I have learned that kangaroos and koalas live in Australia.*
  - *I have learned that Australia is both a country and a continent.*

- Read the book again and look for the vocabulary words.
  - *I see the word **deserts** on page 13, and the words **coral reefs** on page 20. The other glossary words are found on pages 22 and 23.*

Australia is a country.

It is surrounded by water.

Australia is also a **continent**.

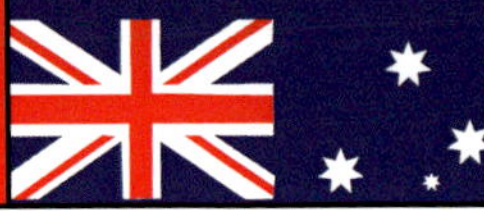

Canberra is Australia's **capital**.

Many tall mountains are near it.

Australia is the only country on Earth that covers a whole continent.

Sydney is the biggest city by population, or the number of people who live there.

The Sydney Harbour Bridge is one of the longest bridges in the world.

The Sydney Opera House is a famous building.

People watch performances there.

Australia has beautiful beaches.

Bondi Beach is in Sydney.

Surfers enjoy the waves.

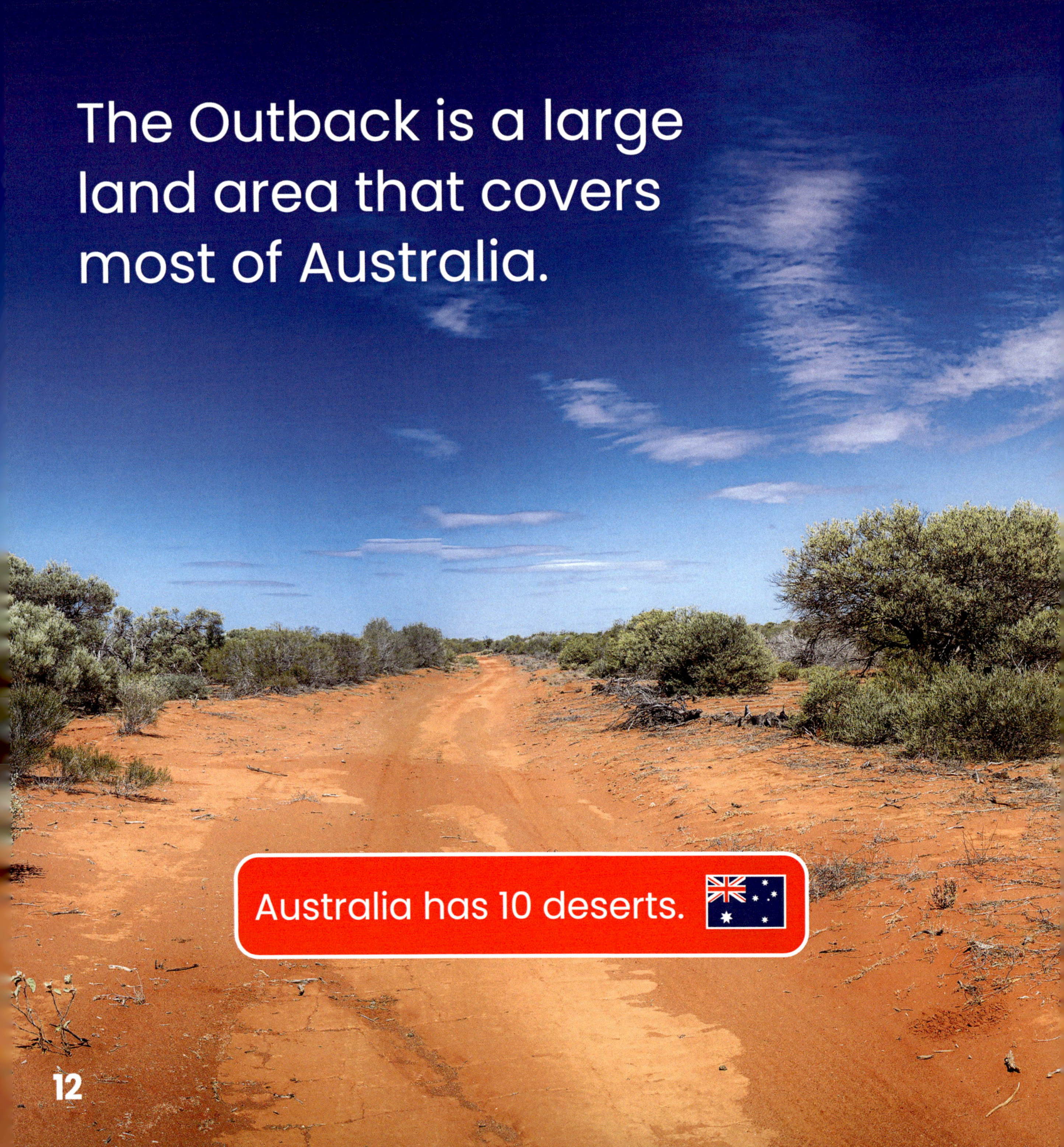

The Outback is a large land area that covers most of Australia.

Australia has 10 deserts.

Its **deserts** are very hot in the summer. Few people live there.

Uluṟu is a giant rock in the Outback.

Uluṟu is special to the Aṉangu people.

The Aṉangu are an **Aboriginal** people.

Australia has **unique** animals. Kangaroos hop in the Outback.

Koalas live in **eucalyptus** forests.

They eat the green leaves.

Koalas spend most of their lives in trees. They rarely come down to the ground.

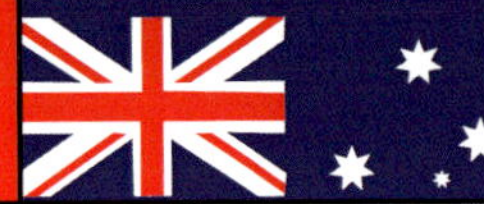

The Great Barrier Reef is under the sea near Australia.

It is the largest **coral reef** in the world.

Colorful fish swim there.

Australia is a special country!

Glossary

Aboriginal (a-bor-I-juh-nuhl): In Australia, the term used for the first people known to have lived in an area

capital (KAP-i-tl): The city where the government of a country or a state is located

continent (KON-tuh-nuhnt): One of seven main land areas on Earth

coral reef (CO-ruhl REEF): A hard underwater structure made up of the skeletons of tiny sea creatures

desert (DEH-zert): A very hot, dry area that gets a small amount of rain per year

eucalyptus (yoo-kuh-LIP-tus): A tree that naturally grows in Australia and on nearby islands

unique (yoo-NEEK): Very special and unlike anything else

Index

About the Author

Tracy Vonder Brink

Tracy Vonder Brink loves to visit new places. She has never been to Australia, but she has held a baby kangaroo. She lives in Cincinnati with her husband, two daughters, and two rescue dogs.

Crabtree Publishing

crabtreebooks.com 800-387-7650

Published in Canada
Crabtree Publishing
616 Welland Avenue
St. Catharines, Ontario
L2M 5V6

Published in the United States
Crabtree Publishing
347 Fifth Avenue
Suite 1402-145
New York, NY 10016

Written by: Tracy Vonder Brink

Photo Credits: Richie Chan: cover; Irina Sokolovskaya: p. 3; Greg Grave: p. 5; Rudy Balasko: p. 6-7; Chris Howey: p. 9(top); Janvon Uxkull Gyllenboard: p. 9 (bottom); Tara Vyshnya: p. 11; Wright Out There: p. 12-13; StickyBeakTV: p. 14; JMundy: p. 15; Luke Shelley: p. 17; Robert LaRosa: p. 17; Debra James: p. 21

Hardcover 978-1-0396-4456-4
Paperback 978-1-0396-4647-6

Library and Archives Canada
Cataloguing in Publication
Available at the Library and Archives Canada

Library of Congress
Cataloging-in-Publication Data
Available at the Library of Congress

Printed in the U.S.A./112023/PP20230920